Gift Aid item

Dear Reader,

Welcome to this special spiritual journey designed to get our hearts ready for the joyous Resurrection celebration. This book is a personalized guide to help you through the days of Lent, written just for you. Together, we will ponder various facets of our religion throughout this time, learning from Scripture's wisdom, motivational sayings, and real-world struggles.

Every day of this journey offers a fresh perspective on spiritual principles that will deepen your understanding of God, yourself, and other people. We think that these times of concentration, introspection, and prayer will be beneficial to you and will ready your heart for the delight of the Resurrection.

Grow, learn, and get experience. As you journey on your own path to a deeper relationship with God, let this book be your guide and companion. Savor every day of Lent, be open to a fresh understanding of faith, and give this special occasion your whole attention.

With blessings,

Author

Day 1

"Preparing for Lent"

"Watch therefore, for you don't know the day nor the hour in which the Son of Man is coming " Matthew 25:13

Let's consider "Devotion" as we approach Lent. It is more than just waiting; it is an active preparedness and centering of the heart on God's ways. During Lent, one should be receptive to the mysteries that God may choose to reveal and to the invisible.

Our whole self should be prepared for the task at hand—mind, heart, and hands. Like the wise men who were anticipating the arrival of a star, we too must be actively engaged in our spiritual path. Now is the time to set our hearts open to receive the Holy Spirit's inspirations and to ready our hands to act in obedience and love.

Reflections:

What specific actions can we do to actively get ready for Lent?

....

How can "Devotion" go beyond just waiting around?

....

Which spiritual practices can assist us in preparing ourselves for God's plans for our lives?

....

How might this preparedness affect how we view the unknowable future?

....

Challenge:

Find a quiet moment, make a list of precise objectives and promises, and be ready to confront invisible obstacles through prayer, almsgiving, or other acts of kindness to proactively prepare your heart for Lent.

Day 2

"Abstaining from Sacrifice; Remembering Mercy"

"But you go and learn what this means: 'I desire mercy, and not sacrifice'"

Matthew 9,13

On this second day of Lent, let's take a closer look at "Abstaining from Sacrifice; Remembering Mercy" Proverbs tells us that showing mercy requires more than just putting it off; it also requires deliberate consideration and application.

Refusing to make a sacrifice does not imply passivity; rather, it is a decision to emphasize kindness of heart. During Lent, our sacrifices take on a new significance as opportunities to be generous to others. We must behave with empathy, understanding, and a readiness to actively show mercy to people who are in need right now.

Reflections:

Practicing Mercy: What acts of kindness may we do for others throughout Lent?

....

Effect on Sacrifice: How does mercy influence the kind and strength of our offerings?

....

Balance and Advantages: What are the advantages of finding a middle ground between showing mercy and forgoing sacrifice?

....

Challenge:

This day, find a chance to do something specifically kind for someone who is in need. Allow your deeds to serve as a living example of the "remember mercy" principle, providing comfort and encouragement to others throughout this Lenten season.

Day 3

"Hope Overcomes Fear"

"I have told you these things, that in me you may have peace. In the world you have trouble; but cheer up! I have overcome the world." John 16:33

On this third day of Lent, let's concentrate on the themes of "Fear and Hope". Jesus tells us in the Gospel of John that hope is strong and can conquer all fears.

We frequently battle a variety of fears in our daily lives, from worries about loved ones to dread about the future. Nevertheless, Jesus claims that since He has conquered the world, we too have triumphed over fear. In addition to being a foundation for hope, this is a promise.

Reflections:

Daily Fears: What impact do our day-to-day anxieties have on our spiritual lives? How might these fears be offset by hope in Jesus?

....

God's Promises: Consider the assurances that God has provided for us in the Bible. In the face of challenges, which of these promises can give you hope?

....

How can we encourage others to have hope, especially those who are facing uncertainty and fear?

....

Challenge:

Spend some time candidly discussing your thoughts about Lent with a friend, emphasizing the importance of overcoming fear and cultivating hope. Let this dialogue serve as a means of encouraging one another, fortifying one another's faith and fortifying our hope.

Day 4

"Discovering beauty in repentance"

"Behold, I am with you always, even to the end of the age. " Matthew 28:20

On the fourth day of Lent, let's take some time today to focus on "Discovering Beauty in Repentance." Jesus says that He will be with us always, even on the days that appear hard and call for repentance.

Finding the beauty in our flaws is a journey that goes along with having times of regret. Now is the moment to consider repentance as a chance to gain a deeper understanding of who we are and how we relate to God. Embracing shame as a means of transformation can help us find new sides to ourselves and feel God's presence during trying times.

Reflections:

The Process of Repentance: How can we reframe repentance so that we might find beauty in it?

....

Transformation by Humiliation: What are the advantages of accepting repentance as a means of bringing about change?

....

Blessing in Difficulty: Can we recognize the lessons that come from and the blessings that lie behind challenging circumstances?

....

Challenge:

Spend some time today considering repentance as a way to find beauty in our life. To develop a deeper relationship with Jesus, look for opportunities that challenge you to ponder and pray. By doing so, you will learn to recognize His presence even in trying circumstances.

Day 5

"The Power of Unity in Prayer"

"Again, assuredly I tell you, that if two of you will agree on earth concerning anything that they will ask, it will be done for them by my Father who is in heaven." Matthew 18:19

On the fifth day of Lent, I want to focus on "The Power of Unity in Prayer" and discuss how praying together can deepen spiritual ties and improve relationships.

Jesus highlights in his teachings the efficacy of a prayer that comes from two hearts joined by a single goal. This appeal for prayer unanimity is based on a profound understanding and empathy for one another's needs, not only a consensus on the subject matter of prayer.

Reflections:

The Power of Common Prayer: When you were a member of a cohesive group, how did you personally witness the power of prayer?

....

Heart Consent: What obstacles can one face in order to obtain heart consent while in prayer? How can we get past them to increase the effectiveness of prayer?

....

Restoring Unity: What role can prayer play in bringing people back together in their homes, communities, and worldwide? How may prayer help us be instruments of reconciliation?

....

Challenge:

Spend some time today praying more intently with a group or individual. As we witness the efficacy of collective prayer, let us seek to cultivate peace and unity in our interpersonal relationships as well as inside ourselves.

Day 6

"Mercy in Lent"

"Blessed are the merciful, for they shall obtain mercy." Matthew 5:7

On this sixth day of Lent, we want to take a closer look at "Mercy in Lent" since it is a gift that reconciles and heals our relationships with God and one another.

In His teachings, Jesus promises that those who extend mercy will also be blessed and blessed. This call to contemplation prompts us to consider mercy in a number of contexts, including self-mercy, interpersonal relationships, and repentance.

Reflections:

Mercy toward Self: In light of the challenges we face on a daily basis, how may we show ourselves mercy?

....

Relationships and Mercy: How does showing mercy impact our relationships with others? How might we become a link for God's kindness to other people?

....

Repentance vs. Mercy: How do these two concepts interact in our spiritual development?

....

Challenge:

Seek for a chance today to extend extra kindness to someone. It might be a supportive remark, a helpful hand, or an act of compassion. By showing mercy to others, we strengthen ties of reconciliation and draw nearer to Christ, the ultimate example of mercy.

Day 7

"Joy in Sharing with Others"

"… and to remember the words of the Lord Jesus, that he himself said, 'It is more blessed to give than to receive.'" Acts 20:35

As we approach the seventh day of Lent, we want to take a closer look at the theme of "Joy in Sharing with Others." Acts of the Apostles describes Jesus' teachings as a light that illuminates the delight of giving freely to others.

Jesus tells us that true joy comes from having a kind heart and being able to contribute both materially and emotionally with others, even if in today's world value is frequently determined by worldly goods.

Reflections:

The Joy of Sharing: When you give away material goods or your time and attention to others, what feelings of happiness do you experience?

....

Generosity of Heart: What role does heartfelt generosity play in fostering happiness on the inside as well as the outside? How can we teach ourselves to be generous?

....

Blessings in Sharing: In what ways can giving and receiving be blessed while sharing with others?

....

Challenge:

Seek out an intentional moment today to give generously to others. Allow it to be a manifestation of your happiness in giving, and feel the blessings that come from sharing with those you share it with.

Day 8

"Peace in Inner Silence"

"And the peace of God, which surpasses all understanding, will guard your hearts and your thoughts in Christ Jesus" Philippians 4:7

On the eighth day of Lent, we would want to delve into the theme of "Peace in Inner Silence" drawing inspiration from the words found in the Letter to the Philippians. These words invite us to seek inner silence as a means of achieving a tranquility that is beyond conventional comprehension.

Silence within oneself becomes a guide toward a serenity that transcends this world of noise and chaos.

Reflections:

Inner silence: When you practice moments of inner silence, what feelings of calm do you experience?

....

Peace Beyond understanding: In what ways does the peace mentioned in the Letter to the Philippians go beyond our common perceptions and comprehension of it?

....

Protecting the Heart and Thoughts: In what ways does the practice of inner stillness support the Christian concept of protecting the heart and thoughts?

....

Challenge:

Find some quiet time inside yourself today. Seek a calm place in Christ by immersing yourself in a serene presence in a quiet environment. You will notice when you experience this inner calm that it brings profound harmony and protects your mind and heart.

Day 9

"Living in the Light of God's Love"

"A new commandment I give to you, that you love one another. Just as I have loved you, you also love one another." John 13:34

The theme for our reflection on the ninth day of Lent is "Living in the Light of God's Love." Jesus demonstrates for us in the Gospel of John how God's love for us should be reflected in our love for others.

God's love serves as the cornerstone around which our relationships are constructed in a world where difficulties are a common occurrence. It's an unconditional love that is kind and willing to give up all for you.

Reflections:

Divine Love: How have you personally felt the love of God? How does it show up in your interactions with other people?

………………………………………………

Empathy: How can we show people the same love that Jesus showed us? What impact does His example have on our day-to-day interactions?

………………………………………………

Fruits of Love: For ourselves and everyone we come in contact with, what are the benefits of living in the light of God's love?

………………………………………………

Challenge:

Show them your love and affection actively today. Allow God's love penetrate your decisions, actions, and words. Think about the ways you can spread God's love to those around you by loving people like Jesus did.

Day 10

"Discovering Treasures in the Silence of the Heart"

"For where your treasure is, there will your heart be also. " Luke 12:34

This tenth day of Lent, let's take some time to consider "Discovering Treasures In The Silence Of Deepest Heart." According to what Jesus says in Luke's Gospel, the most valuable things are frequently concealed in the quiet places of our souls, where nothing is spoken.

Living in a noisy, stimulating world frequently interferes with our capacity to lose oneself in the inner calm, which is where the real treasures are kept secret.

Reflections:

Treasures of the Heart: What priceless items do you have stashed away in your heart? Can you see how important silence within yourself is to finding them?

....

Creative Silence: How may being silent affect your capacity for original thought and life discovery?

....

Values of Treasures: Which principles are most significant to you? Do they align with your innermost thoughts and feelings?

....

Challenge:

Spend some time today just being in your own heart's silence. Locate a peaceful area where you may de-stress and give yourself permission to discover the treasures that are hidden deep within your soul. Allow yourself to reflect on the importance and beauty of inner quiet during this time.

Day 11

"Trusting in the Passing Moment"

"Therefore don't be anxious for tomorrow, for tomorrow will be anxious for itself"

Matthew 6:34

The topic for reflection for the eleventh day of Lent is "Trusting in the Passing Moment." Jesus tells us in Matthew's Gospel to trust in the here and now and not to lose our peace of mind over an uncertain future.

Worries about the future can consume our spirits in the fast-paced, unpredictable world of today. But there's also profound wisdom in these statements from Christ: every moment has its own difficulties, but it also conceals something special

.

Reflections:

Future Concerns: What obstacles do you face as a result of your anxieties about the future? How do these anxieties impact your day-to-day activities?

....

Trust: How does having a trusting relationship impact your ability to feel at ease during uncertain times?

....

Transient Moment: In spite of the uncertainty of tomorrow, how can we find happiness and contentment in the here and now?

....

Challenge:

Remind yourself that the true power is found in believing God in the here and now, whenever you start to feel the strain of worry for the future. By exercising trust and finding serenity in the fleeting moment, you can fully engage in the present.

Day 12

"Purifying the Heart in Grace"

"Create in me a clean heart, O God"

Psalm 51:10

On the twelfth day of Lent, we are prompted to consider the subject of "Purifying the Heart In Grace." Psalm 51 articulates the desire to restore one's relationship with God and purify one's heart.

We frequently forget about our spiritual needs in the daily chaos of life. It is worthwhile to pause during this time of conversion and repentance and examine your heart.

Reflections:

The Purification Need: Where in your life do you sense a need for a heart renewal and purification? Which transgressions or trying circumstances are preventing you from reaching God?

....

God's cleansing grace: In what ways might it be a means of healing and purification? How may its work be felt in our daily lives?

....

New Heart: In relationships with God and others, what are the advantages of possessing a "pure heart"?

....

Challenge:

Set aside some time today to consciously pray for the purity of your heart. Pray to God for the grace that purifies, heals, and brings life back to its fullest. Allow God's grace to transform your heart. Be open to receiving it.

Day 13

"Growing in Patience and Perseverance"

"… that you won't be sluggish, but imitators of those who through faith and perseverance inherited the promises" Hebrews 6,12

The topic for thought on the thirteenth day of Lent is "Growing in Patience and Perseverance."

Time pressure is pushed to every aspect of our life in today's fast-paced society, making patience and endurance essential traits. They not only stand for moral principles, but they also provide a means of learning deeper truths about our relationships with God and others.

Reflections:

The Importance of Patience: What difficulties do you encounter when exercising patience? How does patience help one comprehend people and situations more truly?

....

Spiritual Perseverance: What is the impact of enduring in spiritual activities such as prayer on your spiritual development?

....

Patience as a Tool for Transformation: In what ways may patience aid in character development and transformation?

....

Challenge:

Whenever you find yourself in a circumstance that calls for patience today, take a time to reflect on the lessons that can be learned. Strive to tackle challenges with patience and an open mind to the possibilities of spiritual development

Day 14

"Love in Action"

" Let love be without hypocrisy. Abhor that which is evil. Cling to that which is good." Romans 12:9

On this fourteenth day of Lent, we are prompted to consider "Love in Action." The emphasis in the Letter to the Romans is on how true love shows up in deeds and attitudes toward right and wrong.

In light of the fact that fasting is a period during which we actively seek to become closer to God and our neighbors as well as to renounce something, let's reflect on whether or not our love is genuine, grounded, and producing positive results.

It's important to think about whether we always behave and make decisions out of love, or if there are moments when our love is only words with no real repercussions. Can we find evil and detest it while clinging to what is good?

Reflections:

Love in regular Actions: What choices and deeds do you do that show love on a regular basis? How may the smallest gestures and behaviors be used to build love?

....

Disgust with Evil: Which behaviors align with love and which go against its essence? How do we separate ourselves from all evil in order to manifest love?

....

Kindness to Others: How can you show love to people in your immediate vicinity in a practical way?

....

Challenge:

Attempt to be conscious of your choices and actions today. Think about whether they actually align with love or whether they may use some work. Put in place tangible measures to show love in action, trying to do good wherever you can.

Day 15

"Living in Integrity"

"All the paths of Yahweh are loving kindness and truth" Psalm 25:10

For our fifteenth day of Lent, we are asked to consider "Living in Integrity." Psalm 25 serves as a reminder that love and truth are the cornerstones of true living.

It is important to consider whether our lives are in line with our inner beliefs and being honest with ourselves in the modern world when we frequently comply with societal pressures and external expectations.

Living with integrity entails sticking to one's principles despite the difficulties the outside world throws at us. It also entails leading an honest life and establishing sincere connections with people.

Reflections:

Being Sincere with Yourself: What choices do you make to be sincere with yourself in your life? How does being honest affect your mindset and decisions?

....

Faithfulness to the Truth: In your interactions with other people, how do you show faithfulness to the truth? How can you foster trust and authenticity in your surroundings?

....

Love and Truth: In your life, how do love and truth interact? How do these two principles combine to mold your personality and affect the people you interact with?

....

Challenge:

Count the integrity in your life as of right now. Think about whether the things you do and say are consistent with your true self and beliefs.

Day 16

"Humility before God"

"The result of humility and the fear of Yahweh is wealth, honor, and life"

Proverbs 22:4

On this happy sixteenth day of Lent, we are prompted to consider "Humility before God." Proverbs tells us that the path to abundance, respect, and a fulfilled life is humility.

It is worthwhile to consider the significance of humility in our lives in the modern world, where ambition is frequently encouraged. Are we prepared to humble ourselves before God, accept His counsel, and own our limitations?

Reflections:

Relationships and humility: What effects does humility have on your relationships with other people? What are some ways that you can act and speak humble?

....

Acceptance of limitations: What are the advantages of acknowledging your limitations? How is humility a route to one's own development?

....

Prayer and Humility: How do you pray with humility? How may a location of humility and dedication be a meeting point with God through prayer?

....

Challenge:

Make an effort to be more humble in your interactions and choices today. Take some time to consider your own shortcomings and develop an open mind to whatever lessons God may choose to impart via humble prayer.

Day 17:

"Sharing Joy"

"My heart has trusted in him, and I am helped. Therefore my heart greatly rejoices." Psalm 28:7

The theme for the seventeenth day of Lent is "Sharing Joy." Psalm 28 reminds us that the joy we experience together has the capacity to spread to others in addition to ourselves.

Sharing joy becomes a gift that we may provide to one another in today's hectic world, where we frequently confront numerous obstacles, offering respite and revitalization.

Reflections:

Joyful Sources: In what aspect of your life do you find joy? What experiences and moments bring you the most joy?

....

Joy Sharing: How can we spread our happiness to others? Which particular actions make other individuals smile?

....

Effects of Joy Sharing: What are the effects of joy sharing on our relationships and those around us? How can we help others feel good about themselves?

....

Challenge:

Attempt to make someone else smile today. Give everyone you meet a smile, an optimistic outlook on life, or a brief moment of happiness. You could be surprised by the influence of your happiness.

Day 18

"Truth in Silence"

""Speak; for your servant hears." Samuel 3,10

This 18th day of Lent invites us to consider "Truth in Silence." Samuel reminds us that even in the midst of complete silence, truth can exist and that our quiet can serve as an homage to God's holiness.

Being silent in the cacophonous world of today can be a priceless gift. Sometimes the greatest beauty and insight can be found in solitude.

Reflections:

Truth in silence: During your silence, what truths do you uncover? How can one reflect and have a self-encounter in silence?

....

Homage to Truth: In what ways might our silence honor the truth? How can worshiping God's knowledge and perfection be accomplished through silence?

....

Relationships and Silence: What impact does silence have on our interpersonal relationships? Can quiet reveal truth in our relationships with those we love?

....

Challenge:

Today, find the truth in quiet by being silent for a little while. It can be a quick prayer, a period of introspection, or a pause to consider what is most important to you. There are moments when silence speaks louder than words.

Day 19

"Listening from the Heart"

"so as to turn your ear to wisdom, and apply your heart to understanding" Proverbs 2,2

The theme of Lent's nineteenth day is "Listening from the Heart." The passages from the Proverbs serve as a reminder that genuine unity with God arises from sincere hearing what He has to say.

It becomes crucial to be able to focus on God's voice in the noisy environment of today. One of the keys to experiencing union with God and drawing nearer to Him is often listening from the heart.

Reflections:

Listening from the Heart: In the modern society, what obstacles do you encounter while trying to listen from the heart? What actions can we do to strengthen our capacity to hear God and His word?

....

Unity with God: What role does heartfelt listening have in bringing about unity with God? How can we put listening into practice and action in our day-to-day activities?

....

Relationships and listening: What impact does hearing from the heart have on our interpersonal relationships? Can we prioritize listening so that we can be more aware of and receptive to the needs of others?

....

Challenge:

Take a moment today to focus and be silent for yourself. As you listen from the heart, pay attention to God's voice speaking to you in your heart and to the intricacies of life. Spend time in prayer, asking God to grant you the capacity to pay attention.

Day 20

"Beauty of Emotion"

"But the fruit of the Spirit is love, joy, peace, patience, kindness, goodness, faith"

Galatians 5,22

Today, on the twentieth day of Lent, we are prompted to consider "The Beauty of Emotion." The Galatians serve as a reminder that the genuine richness of life can be found in the depths of emotion.

It might be a gift to ourselves and others to take a minute in today's hectic life to appreciate beauty and emotion.

Reflections:

The Beauty of Emotion: When in your life did you feel deeply? How can we become more conscious of and receptive to the beauty all around us?

……………………………………………………

Life Richtness: What role do feelings play in making our life richer? Can we find beauty in the mundane, ordinary moments?

……………………………………………………

Emotion in Action: How may the beauty of emotion be mobilized? Can we spread this abundance and encourage others to find beauty in their own lives?

……………………………………………………

Challenge:

Challenge: Immerse yourself in a situation that makes you feel deeply emotional today. It may be a prayer moment, a piece of art, or music. By expressing your feelings and encouraging people to appreciate life's beauty, you can spread this beauty to others.

Day 21

"Trust in God's Plans"

"Trust in Yahweh with all your heart, and don't lean on your own understanding"

Proverbs 3:5

The focus of Lent on day twenty-first is "Trust in God's Plans." We are encouraged to completely trust God by the words of Proverbs 3:5, especially when it comes to His plans for our lives.

Although life frequently throws us with different obstacles, having faith in God's purposes can bring comfort and assurance.

Reflections:

Putting Your Trust in God's Plans: Determine which decisions need your faith in God. How can you submit to His will in the face of conflicting plans?

....

The Role of Trust in Life: How Does Believing in God's Plans Impact Everyday Choices? How may this trust help to promote calm during tumultuous times?

....

Relationships and Trust: What Effect Does Relationship Trust Have on God's Plans? How can you use this confidence to social situations?

....

Challenge:

Give your plans to God in prayer today. Have faith in His flawless plans, even if they diverge from yours. Allow Him to lead you, and seek knowledge to comprehend His purposes for your life.

Day 22

"The Power of Forgiveness"

"And be kind to one another, tender hearted, forgiving each other, just as God also in Christ forgave you" Ephesians 4:32

This year, as the twenty-second day of Lent draws near, we would like to focus especially on the "Power of Forgiveness." This crucially important part of our spiritual path guides us toward profound divine love and has a profound effect on how we relate to others.

Reflections:

The Power of Forgiveness: Using Christ as God's example, how do you comprehend and engage in the act of forgiveness?

....

Change of the Heart: How does it impact the environment of God's love and your relationships with others?

....

Relationship Forgiveness: What obstacles do you encounter while attempting to provide forgiveness to others? In what ways could forgiving one another manifest God's love in your day-to-day existence?

....

Challenge:

Identify any circumstances where you can exercise forgiveness today. Transcend your emotions to God via prayer, allowing God to fill you from the inside out with his abiding love and opening your heart to the power of forgiveness.

Day 23:

"Trust in the Invisible Signposts."

"Trust in Yahweh with all your heart, and don't lean on your own understanding"

Proverbs 3:5

As the twenty-third day of Lent approaches, we would like to concentrate on the subject of "Trust in Invisible Signposts." This is a crucial part of our spiritual journey that directs our life and points us in the direction of God's flawless, unseen methods.

God has unseen signs hidden everywhere in our lives that point us in the direction of His ideal plan. But occasionally, these pathways are not always evident to us as humans, necessitating a great deal of confidence. We must challenge ourselves to submit to God's guidance even when we are unable to see the entire way ahead when faced with life's uncertainties and times when our plans go through.

Reflections:

Trust in God's Plans: What are some ways that you use your faith to guide your decisions in life? When your intentions collide with reality, how do you still do what He says?

....

The Role of Trust in Life: How does having faith in God's plans impact your day-to-day choices and dispositions?

....

Relationships and Trust: How does having faith in God's plans impact your relationships with others? How can we apply this trust to our relationships with friends, family, and coworkers?

....

Challenge:

Spend today in prayer and giving God control over your goals and aspirations. Even though His plans don't always fit your expectations, have faith that they are excellent. Ask for insight in comprehending God's plans for you and offer your heart to Him for direction.

Day 24

"Hope in the Darkness"

"'I am the light of the world. He who follows me will not walk in the darkness, but will have the light of life." John 8:12

As the twenty-fourth day of Lent approaches, we would like to take some time to consider "Hope in the Darkness." In the depths of our despair, hope is found in the light of Christ, which proclaims His triumph over death.

May this hope, stemming from His promise of eternal life, be a source of strength and perseverance for us in the face of difficulties. When we open ourselves to this light, we become His witnesses in a world that is often drowning in the darkness of unbelief, evil and despair.

Reflections:

Feeling Hope: In what ways has hope been present for you in trying times? What impact has this hope had on the way you view hardship and obstacles?

....

Spreading Hope to Others: What are some ways that we might help others see hope? How can we brighten the lives of those who are in the dark with our faith and hope?

....

Hope and Daily Decisions: What role does hope play in your day-to-day choices? How do we live out this hope by making decisions that align with what Jesus taught?

....

Challenge:

Think about how you can give someone hope in their life today. Stay receptive to chances to spread love and hope, serving as a lighthouse for others in the shadow of Christ.

Day 25:

"Conscious Love"

"let's not love in word only, or with the tongue only, but in deed and truth." John 3:18

Our goal for today's contemplation is to delve deeper into the concept of "Conscious Love." Let's explore how love can be expressed via our deeds in a genuine way that transcends words and becomes a physical embodiment of our spiritual journey.

Conscious Love guides us toward a way of living in which the profound love that wells up in our emotions is expressed via our deeds. This is the transference of love to the tangible realities of everyday life—it is more than just statements or pledges.

Reflections:

Transferring Love from Words to Deeds: What are some practical ways that we might put our love into deeds? What doable acts can we take to align our behavior with love?

....

Love as a Transformative Force: What effects may conscious love have on our environments and interpersonal relationships? How can we spot situations where empathy and compassion are needed?

....

The Holy Spirit's Practice of Love: How Can the Holy Spirit Assist Us in Manifesting Conscious Love? How might we live our life with greater receptivity to His inspiration?

....

Challenge:

Challenge: Today, pause before acting or reacting, and ask yourself if what you're doing is consistent with the idea of conscious love. Make a conscious effort to act with true affection and concern.

Day 26

"Joy in Humiliation"

"Yahweh's blessing brings wealth, and he adds no trouble to it." Proverbs 10:22

We are on day twenty-six of Lent. Our focus for today will be on the theme of "Joy in Humiliation."Oftentimes, things that seem like a source of guilt at first can actually offer us true joy if we are open to receiving God's blessing.

Let us discover what joy looks like when we are humble and trust in God's plan. Disgrace can be a catalyst for a deeper connection with God as we realize that His abundance surpasses whatever challenges we face.

Reflections:

The Secret of Joy: How Can Humility Help Us Find Joy During Challenging Times? How can we live humble lives given everything God has planned for us?

....

God's Grace Despite Disgrace: What challenges or humiliations have you gone through that have ended up being a source of blessings from God? How can we grow to trust His intentions?

....

Happiness in Service: How can helping others make you happy, even in the face of challenges?

....

Challenge:

Identify anything that you feel is embarrassing or difficult for you today. Take a minute to express gratitude to God for the lessons learned from these encounters and to allow yourself to be joyfully blessed by God.

Day 27:

"Living in Thanksgiving."

"… giving thanks always concerning all things in the name of our Lord Jesus Christ to God, even the Father " Ephesians 5:20

This day of Lent, the twenty-seventh, we would like to talk about the theme of "Living in Thanksgiving." The power of gratitude, which changes our hearts and opens the door to a deeper relationship with God, is concealed within the day-to-day difficulties and delights.

Let's explore how cultivating gratitude might change our life and increase our receptivity to God's grace. When we have gratitude in our hearts, we can see beauty in the ordinary and grow closer to God.

Reflections:

Gratitude in Tough Times: How Might Giving Thanks Help Us Through Difficulties? How can we locate the things for which we are thankful even under trying circumstances?

....

Gratitude as a Way of Life: In what ways may cultivating thankfulness serve as a kind of prayer? In what ways may giving thanks improve our connection with God?

....

Giving Thanks for the blessings of the Holy Spirit: How may we express our gratitude for the blessings that the Holy Spirit has given us? In what ways do these gifts advance our spiritual development?

....

Challenge:

Make it a point to express gratitude every single day starting today. Take a moment to reflect on the things for which you are grateful to God today.

Day 28

"Participation in Suffering"

"When one member suffers, all the members suffer with it. When one member is honored, all the members rejoice with it"

1 Corinthians 12:26

As we approach the twenty-eighth day of Lent, we would like to consider the theme of "Participation in Suffering." Being conscious of the pain of others is essential to the Christian experience, and by comprehending Jesus' suffering, fasting enables us to approach the mystery of salvation.

Reflections:

Sharing the Pain of Others: What actions can we take to knowingly contribute to the pain of others? How can we be there for people at difficult times, offering our support and presence?

....

The Value of Pain in the Context of Redemption: How do we interpret our own experiences of pain in relation to Jesus' agony on the cross? Seeing as how Jesus endured our pain, what hope is left for us?

....

Challenge of Solidarity: Think about ways you may show others that you support their pain more today. Donate your time, your prayers, or practical assistance to those in need.

Recall that sharing in pain can serve as a witness to the hope and love that come from our religion.

Day 29

"The Light of Salvation"

"Again, therefore, Jesus spoke to them, saying, "I am the light of the world. He who follows me will not walk in the darkness, but will have the light of life."" John 8:12

We would want to take some time today, the twenty-ninth day of Lent, to think more deeply on the "Light of Salvation." In addition to being our constant light, Jesus Christ serves as a guide, bringing us from the darkness of life's struggles into the brightness of eternal. We can navigate even the darkest parts of our lives with His light because He is our assurance in uncertainty.

Reflections:

Light in the Darkness: How can Jesus be a light to help you navigate the dark?

....

Shine As Saved: What ways can we show people the love of salvation? How can we illuminate the path for those who are still seeking it with our words and deeds?

....

Meeting the Light: In what ways might we purposefully meet Jesus as our light? Which spiritual disciplines aid in maintaining our connection to the light's source?

....

Challenge:

Today, make time for a face-to-face meeting with Jesus, the source of salvation. Let the light of God shine within you via prayer and scripture meditation. Next, seek out chances to tenderly and empathetically impart this light to others.

Day 30

"The Light of Hope"

"In him was life, and the life was the light of men. The light shines in the darkness, and the darkness hasn't overcome it" John 1: 4-5

As we enter the thirtyth day of Lent, we would like to take some time to consider the "Light of Hope." The source of life and light that shines through life's darkness and gives us unending hope is Jesus Christ.

Jesus is that unending Light, and the Glow of Hope is like the rising sun, eradicating the darkness. No matter how black our roads may be, they are illuminated by the source that we encounter with Him.

Reflections:

Hope among Difficulties: In what ways does Christ, the Glimmer of Hope, assist you throughout challenging circumstances? Think about the particular instances that demonstrate His existence in your life.

....

Eliminating the Darkness: What role may we play in spreading the Glimmer of Hope to those in our immediate vicinity?

....

Believing in the Source of Light: Consider how you can deepen your relationship with Jesus, the Glimmer of Hope, via prayer and meditation.

....

Challenge:

Concentrate on spreading hope to everyone around you today. proactively look for chances to lend others your help and good vibes. Let your beacon of hope shine through your compassionate deeds, illuminating Christ as the source of unfailing hope.

Day 31

"Oasis of Inner Peace"

"Yahweh is my shepherd; I shall lack nothing. He makes me lie down in green pastures. He leads me beside still waters" Psalm 23: 1-2

This reflection, on the thirty-first day of Lent, will center around the "Oasis of Inner Calm." We all have times in our spiritual lives when we need to take a break, take a deep breath, and find an oasis of inner serenity.

Take a moment to visualize peaceful waterways and verdant pastures guided by the Shepherd. You can find respite here, where you can lose yourself in quiet, sense God's presence, and regain your strength.

Reflections:

Looking for an Oasis: Where in your spiritual life do you sense that you might use some calm and inner serenity? Think about the spiritual activities that can guide you to this peaceful, restful place.

……………………………………………

The Gift of quiet: How may quiet help one discover a haven of inner tranquility?

……………………………………………

Laying Down Our Heads in God's Presence: What Peace Can We Take With Us Into Our Everyday Lives? Think about the effects these times of inner serenity have on your relationships, choices, and mindset.

……………………………………………

Challenge:

Make time today to discover your own quiet haven. Take some quiet time to pray and reflect as you rest. Allow yourself to find inner serenity during this time of rest, and then share that peace with those around you.

Day 32

"Transformation in the Light of Love"

"Love is patient and is kind. Love doesn't envy. Love doesn't brag, is not proud"

1 Corinthians 13:4

On this the thirty-second day of Lent, let's explore the theme of "Transformation in the Light of Love" in today's reflection. St. Paul demonstrates the characteristics of genuine love, which has God's grace as its source.

In our connections with others, St. Paul exhorts us to be kind, patient, and not to take ourselves too seriously. These principles shine a light on our journey toward spiritual enlightenment. The metamorphosis we go through, molding our hearts into the likeness of God's love, comes when we learn to be patient, kind, and humble.

Reflections:

Patience as Strength: When we have patience, we can withstand challenging circumstances. It is evidence of fortitude and empathy.

....

Graciousness in Action: When we are gracious to others, relationships can change for the better. It is the capacity to foster mutual understanding and recognize the good in people.

....

Refusing to take pride enables us to be modest and receptive to God's grace.

....

Challenge:

This day, concentrate on being patient, kind, and humble in your interactions with other people. Take note of how these attitudes impact the environment around you and consider how you may help bring about change by living a loving life.

Day 33

"Crowning Actions of Love"

"But now faith, hope, and love remain - these three. The greatest of these is love."

1 Corinthians 13:13

As we approach the thirty-third day of Lent, let us focus on the theme of "Crowning Actions of Love." According to St. Paul, love has a special position in the Christian life and is even more important than hope and faith.

Love is the pinnacle of our deeds; it is the source of significance for our spiritual pursuits. Love ought to be the most important component of all the tasks we completed during the fasting period. It is what gives our efforts purpose and a clear path to salvation.

Reflections:

Love as the Purpose of Action: How do you interpret love in your Lenten deeds? How may your spiritual endeavors be directed and guided by love?

....

Love's Effects on Life: How has love specifically affected your life? What impact does it have on your decisions, attitudes, and relationships?

....

Crowning the Fasting Effort: By showing love to God and our friends, how may we make the most of our efforts during the fasting season? In what way might love inspire greater spiritual development?

....

Challenge:

Think about how you can center your activities around love today. Seek out tangible occasions to show others your love through both your words and deeds. Let love be the reward for all your hard work this Lent.

Day 34

"Discovering the Treasures of Community"

"Whatever you do, in word or in deed, do all in the name of the Lord Jesus, giving thanks to God the Father through him."

Colossians 3:17

Let's concentrate on the theme of "Discovering the Treasures of Community" on this the thirty-fourth day of Lent. The Christian community is like a gold mine of spiritual gifts, opportunities for encouraging one another, and ways to spread God's love.

Exploring the spiritual wealth inside a community is akin to taking a trip into the treasure chest, where every individual contributes something special. It can be the community's intense prayers, the youthful people's excitement, or the experience of the older members. During this Lenten season, it is important noticing what gifts the Holy Spirit is displaying in your connections with one other.

Reflections:

Community Treasures of the Spirit: What spiritual gems have you found in your neighborhood? In your relationships, which gifts of the Holy Spirit are evident?

....

Mutual Support: During Lent, what instances of mutual support did you encounter in the community? What particular instances demonstrate how valuable you both are to one another?

....

God's Love in Action: What joint efforts can your community make to make God's love evident? How can you share this love with those outside of your own circle?

....

Challenge:

Today, look for concrete ways to discover the treasures of the spirit in your community. Be open to giving and receiving, share the experience of Lent with others. Let your community become a place where you discover and develop the gifts God offers you.

Day 35

"Feelings in Waiting"

"Therefore justice is far from us, and righteousness doesn't overtake us. We look for light, but see darkness; for brightness, but we walk in obscurity." Isaiah 59:9

This 35th day of Lent, we would like to focus on the subject of "Feelings in Waiting." Expectations expressed by the Prophet Isaiah are occasionally met with disappointment. During the waiting phase, how do we handle our emotions, particularly when things don't go as planned?

Reflections:

Feelings of Shock: How do we handle disappointment when life doesn't turn out the way we expected it to? In trying times, how do we find hope?

……………………………………………

Hope Despite the Darkness: There is hope despite the darkness and difficulties. When all around us is darkness, what steps do we take to hold onto hope? How can faith enable us to get past tough emotions and confidently face the future?

……………………………………………

Joy in Expectation: In face of hardship, how may we cultivate joy in anticipation? What are the joys that last beyond fleeting emotions and bolster our faith?

……………………………………………

Challenge:

Consider your sentiments regarding upcoming events for a moment today. Try to be grateful and focus on the good things in life, even when things are tough.

Day 36

"Exploring the Sources of Wisdom"

"Wisdom is supreme. Get wisdom. Yes, though it costs all your possessions, get understanding." Proverbs 4:7

This 36th day of Lent, let's concentrate on the subject of "Seeking the Sources of Wisdom." Wisdom is a treasure that gives you a better grasp of life and aids in decision-making.

It's simple to overlook the profound source of wisdom in the hectic, information-rich world of today. The Book of Proverbs serves as a reminder that wisdom has exceptional worth and that acquiring it is an investment in our personal growth. While wisdom from many sources can mold us in different ways, it's crucial that we handle what we absorb sensibly and thoroughly. Examine your primary sources of insight today to see if they align with the principles that are important to you.

Reflections:

Sources of Wisdom: From what sources do you get guidance on a daily basis? Which wise people offer you the most support?

………………………………………………

Choosing Wisdom: How does wisdom affect the decisions and choices you make on a daily basis? What are the advantages of making decisions based on wisdom, particularly during Lent?

………………………………………………

Wisdom Sharing: Do you impart your knowledge to others? How can we help each other by imparting knowledge and lessons learned from life?

………………………………………………

Challenge:

Take some time today to focus about the knowledge sources in your life. This could involve thinking back on your own life lessons, conversing with mentors, or reading a smart book. Make an effort to put the knowledge you've acquired into practice so that it advances your own development and motivates others.

Day 37

"Forgiveness, the Key to Freedom"

"Above all these things, walk in love, which is the bond of perfection. [15] And let the peace of God rule in your hearts, to which also you were called in one body, and be thankful." Colossians 3: 14-15

The subject for this 37th day of Lent is "Forgiveness, the Key to Freedom." Let's concentrate on this. St. Paul's remarks serve as a reminder that happiness and love are necessary for life to be fully lived.

As we make forgiveness the central theme of our spiritual journey today, let's immerse ourselves in contemplation of its power.

The peace of Christ within our hearts becomes a source of harmony, and the love that the Apostle Paul speaks of demonstrates the path to perfection.

Reflections:

The Power of Forgiveness: In your life, what instances of forgiveness have had the biggest influence? How is freedom and peace possible when forgiveness is involved?

....

Love as an Excellent Bond: How does love turn into an excellent bond? How do we cultivate love in our hearts to produce harmony and peace?

....

Christ's Peace in the Heart: How can we give Christ's peace permission to rule in our hearts? What impact does this inner peace have on our interactions with others and the outside world?

....

Challenge:

Take a moment today to reflect on whether you have any situations in your life when you need to forgive someone or yourself. Let this be the day that forgiveness unlocks the door to freedom.

Day 38

"The Light of Smile"

" A glad heart makes a cheerful face, but an aching heart breaks the spirit."

Proverbs 15:13

On this 38th day of Lent, we would like to go further into the theme of "The Light of Smile," reflecting on the significant influence that a happy heart may have on a multitude of facets of our existence.

A grin, which is the mirror of a happy heart, has the special power to clear the clouds from our minds and provide a ray of sunshine, even in the darkest of circumstances. It has the power to alter the atmosphere around us and infuse our lives with delight, much like a magic filter.

Reflections:

The Power of a Smile: How important do you think a smile is? Have you ever observed how individuals around you might be affected by a smile, which is a positive expression?

....

Happiness of the Heart: What connection is there between the delight you feel and the ideas you're having? Have you ever noticed how a grin can make even the most trying situations seem better?

....

Light in the Darkness: In what sense may a smile illuminate the shadowy areas of life? How can we use the small act of smiling to bring happiness and encouragement to others?

....

Challenge:

Master the art of smiling today. Find something to grin about, even in the face of challenges, and share it with others. Let your grin serve as a beacon of light, illuminating the day for both you and everyone you encounter.

Day 39

"Purification of the Heart, Source of Life"

"Restore to me the joy of your salvation. Uphold me with a willing spirit."

Psalm 51:12

This thirty-ninth day of Lent brings us to consider the theme, "Purification of the Heart, Source of Life." Psalm 51 serves as a reminder to us that we must renew our spirits and purify our souls.

We spend the entire Lenten season in deep introspection and spiritual development.

To prevent contamination of our source of life, we also need to clear our hearts of any negative thoughts, emotions, or behaviors.

Reflections:

The Purification Need: How do unfavorable feelings or ideas impact your life? To revitalize your soul, is there anything you need to purify in your heart?

....

Renewing the Spirit: Can the act of forgiveness, meditation, or prayer help to cleanse the heart?

....

Source of Life: In what way can heart purification turn into a source of life? What are the advantages of having a love-filled, burden-free heart?

....

Challenge:

Give your heart some serious thought today as you ponder on its condition. Determine which areas require purification, and then spend some time in prayer asking God to give you a pure heart and a revitalized soul. Allow this to be a turning point in your spiritual development that opens up a fresh stream of energy.

Day 40

"Resurrection of Life"

"Jesus said to her, "I am the resurrection and the life. He who believes in me will still live, even if he dies."

John 11:25

Now that Lent is almost over, it feels akin to a resurrection following a time of introspection, prayer, and self-denial. The words of Jesus himself, who is the life and the resurrection, are recalled in John's Gospel.

Reflections:

Resurrection in Day-to-Day Living: In your life, what indications of resurrection do you observe? After a period of fasting, is there anything that blooms and comes alive?

....

Religion as a Source of Life: How does your religion impact day-to-day activities? How can you make your faith a stronger source of hope and life?

....

Fresh Starts: After Lent, what fresh starts and awakenings are you going to make in your life? As you develop spiritually, what adjustments would you like to see?

....

Challenge:

Celebrate the hope and joy that come from having faith in Jesus Christ today, on Resurrection Day. I hope that you may find life and motivation in the resurrection of Christ to carry on with your religious path.

In summary, Lent was a singular spiritual experience including introspection, prayer, and self-mutilation. We concentrated on developing a greater appreciation for the importance of love, forgiveness, community, and many other facets of our spiritual lives throughout the course of these 40 days. Every day presented a chance to deepen our bonds with God and one another.

Encouragement from scripture, insightful observations, and realistic difficulties all contributed to strengthening our spiritual ties and our relationship with God. Now, as this time draws to a close, With unabashed excitement and hope, we anticipate the resurrection of life, which is represented by this final day.

I pray that these experiences will be with us always, deepening our bonds with one another, providing us with spiritual resources, and molding our personalities. The conclusion of Lent is merely the beginning of a journey towards ongoing spiritual development and upholding moral principles in day-to-day activities. May the pleasure of the Resurrection always be with us, encouraging us to live more fully according to what Christ taught.

Printed in Great Britain
by Amazon